AF504330

AF504330

THE INFLUENCE OF ADVERTISING'S AFFECTIVE QUALITIES ON CONSUMER RESPONSE*

682-73

Alvin J. Silk** and Terry G. Vavra***

September, 1973

THE INFLUENCE OF ADVERTISING'S AFFECTIVE QUALITIES
ON CONSUMER RESPONSE*

682-73

Alvin J. Silk** and Terry G. Vavra***

September, 1973

.

*An earlier version of this paper was presented at the Association for
Consumer Research/American Marketing Association Conference on "Consumer
Information Processing," University of Chicago, November 1, 1972.
The authors are indebted to Stephen Greyser, Michael Ray, and Peter Wright
for helpful comments. The support of the Marketing Science Institute in
the preparation of this paper is also gratefully acknowledged.

**Sloan School of Management, Massachusetts Institute of Technology

***National Broadcasting Company

This paper will appear as a chapter in G. David Hughes and Michael L. Ray,
eds. Consumer Information Processing. Chapel Hill, N.C.: University of
North Carolina Press, forthcoming in 1974.

ABSTRACT

The subject of "pleasant" and "irritating" advertising has a
long history of controversy involving issues of both management and
public policy. Advertising practitioners and researchers have debated
about the existence and/or the nature of the relationship between
consumers'affective reactions to advertising materials and its effectiveness in altering attitudes or behavior toward the product advertised.
The paper presents a review of viewpoints that have been expressed in
the advertising literatire on the question of how consumers' liking
or disliking of advertising messages is related to the ability of
advertising to achieve its intended commercial purposes. Out of this
emerges what amounts to two different theories about the process and
effects of pleasant and unpleasant advertising. Next, empirical
evidence available from advertising research is examined and found to
be equivocal. A laboratory experiment undertaken to test a series of
hypotheses concerning the effects of "hard" and "soft sell" radio commercials on various hierarchical measures of consumer response is
briefly discussed to illustrate how microtheoretical notions from communications research can be applied in this area.

TABLES OF CONTENTS

INTRODUCTION

This paper is concerned with the question of how the persuasive
impact of advertisements is influenced by the nature of the affective
reactions which advertising stimuli evoke among mass media audiences.
If only because advertising is fundamentally an intrusive element in
their lives, it is inevitable that consumers will find certain kinds of
advertising more acceptable or appealing than others. Advertisers in
their perpetual search for better ways to achieve their communication
objectives have long been interested in such reactions. Ratings of the
"likability" of advertising materials are regularly obtained in copy
testing and related types of studies (e.g. Barban, 1969). However, what
normative implications and value to attach to such measurements are
among advertising's oldest and most controversial subjects. Can an
"irritating" commercial be more effective than a "pleasant" one? Is
it necessary for an ad to be "liked" by consumers in order for it to
influence their purchasing behavior? Do "positive" advertising appeals
have any inherent advantage over "negative" ones? Such questions com-
monly arise in the context of managing advertising campaigns, but they
also have a broader significance. Greyser (1973, p. 3) has recently
pointed out that public criticism of the use of "irritating" advertising
may well make this matter "the next public policy battleground for advertisers." Interestingly, Greyser and Reece (1971, p. 159) found that in
a survey of businessmen's attitudes toward advertising, respondents were
about equally divided in their opinions as to whether or not the most
effective TV commercials are also the most annoying.

Over the years a great many studies have been done on the general subject of consumers' attitudes toward advertising. Much of this work has focused on public opinion of advertising as a social institution which Greyser and Bauer (1966) conclude has remained "remarkably stable" over the past three to four decades. Attention has also been given to what consumers like and don't like about advertising practices and techniques. Lazarsfeld's post war research on radio (1946, 1948) and Steiner's work on television (1963, 1966) provide a good deal of information about audience satisfactions and dissatisfactions with broadcast commercials. The most comprehensive and recent investigation in this tradition is the study sponsored by the American Association of Advertising Agencies and reported in Bauer and Greyser's volume, <u>Advertising in America: The Consumer View</u> (1968). This research offers much valuable insight and a vast amount of data about both consumers' overall judgements of advertising as a social institution and their reactions to specific advertising messages appearing in the major media. Thus, a considerable amount of knowledge has been developed about what consumers find favorable and unfavorable about advertising. By comparison, the matter of how these reactions alter the persuasive impact of advertising appears to have received much less systematic study. As McGuire (1969, p. 192) remarked in reviewing social psychological research on a related subject, it might, at first glance, appear unobjectionable to hypothesize that liking and effectiveness are related in a straightforward positive fashion. It turns out, however, that this proposition has not been uniformly accepted in advertising circles, and in fact, a quite well developed opposing point of view has also been put forth.

The plan of the paper is as follows. First we present a summary and analysis of the viewpoints that have been expressed in the advertising

literature concerning the relationship between consumers' affective
reactions toward advertising stimuli and its persuasive impact. We
identify two conflicting theories about this process and note the key
unresolved issues. Next, relevant empirical studies found in the advertising research literature are reviewed. A laboratory experiment
undertaken to test a set of hypotheses concerning the effects of "hard"
and "soft" sell radio commercials is briefly discussed in the last section
of the paper. Finally, some comments are made concerning further work
in this area.

ADVERTISING THEORIES AND VIEWPOINTS

Advertising literature is replete with moralizing, equivocation, and
conflicting speculation on the subject of how affective reactions to
advertisements are related to the ability of advertising stimuli to achieve
their intended commercial purposes. A careful reading of what has been
written by various advertising psychologists and practitioners over the
years reveals what amounts to two different and competing theories. One
school of thought maintains that a curvilinear relationship exists between
effectiveness and affective reaction: the greater the liking or disliking
of the commercial message, the greater its impact. The other point of
view holds that the relationship is a positive monotonic one: that advertising which evokes "pleasant" or favorable reactions is more effective
than advertising that "irritates" or elicits unpleasant feelings. The
former position has been referred to as the "law of extremes," while the
latter may be labelled as the "superiority-of-the-pleasant" thesis. Both
views are examined in detail below.

The "Law of Extremes" Hypothesis

A number of authors have argued that liking and effectiveness are

valence is less important than intensity of affective reactions. Hence,
it has been claimed that either liked or disliked advertising is more
effective than advertising which arouses an indifferent or emotionally
neutral reaction. This notion came to be known as the "law of extremes"
and has been frequently mentioned in advertising texts. For example,
with reference to radio advertising, Wolfe recommended:

> Plan your commercials around the law of extremes, making
> them either so entertaining that they create an immediate
> pleasurable response or so forceful, aggressive, and repetitious
> that they produce a momentarily unpleasant reaction (Wolfe,
> 1949, p. 482, emphasis added).

Lucas and Britt (1950, p. 380) also refer to this type of relationship in their chapter on broadcast advertising but appeared more reluc-
tant than Wolfe to advocate its normative implications.

Occasionally in discussing this relationship, advertising writers
(e.g., Britt, 1955) have noted that psychological research on emotion
and memory indicates that both the intensity and quality of emotional
factors influence memory (Rapaport, 1961). However, the person who
appears to have been most influential in gaining acceptance for the
concept of a "law of extremes" was Horace Schwerin. Both Wolfe (1949,
p. 484) and Lucas and Britt (1950, p. 381) refer to research by Schwerin
on the liking and remembering of radio commercials as the source of
empirical support for this curvilinear relationship in advertising.
Reproduced in both these works is a figure (credited to Schwerin) depict-
ing a smooth J-shaped curve (that is very nearly U-shaped) relating
"liking and remembrance."[1] See Figure 1 below.

INSERT FIGURE 1 HERE

The history of the Schwerin "curve of remembrance" is of some interest. The December, 1955 issue of the Schwerin Research Corporation's _Bulletin_ gives a brief account of its origins. During World War II, Horace Schwerin was involved in a study of commercials which urged G.I.'s to change their shoes daily. Soldiers' like/dislike reactions were first obtained for a large number of commercials. An experiment was then run wherein various commercials were exposed to different units. The commercials were broadcast in mess halls over public address systems that also carried other program material. A noteworthy feature of the research was the use of an unobtrusive measure of behavioral effect to assess the differential impact of the various commercials. The researchers entered the barracks while the G.I.'s were out on duty and placed an inconspicuous mark on the shoes that had been left behind. The day after the commercial had been broadcast, a check was made to see what proportion of the soldiers had followed the message's recommendations and actually changed their shoes. According to the _Bulletin_, the findings showed that "both the well liked and the disliked messages were more effective than the indifferently received ones, with the liked apparently having somewhat of an edge" (Schwerin Research Corporation, 1955, p. 3). The familiar J-shaped curve was presented with the axes labelled "liking for 'G.I.' Commercials" and "% Changing Shoes." The _Bulletin_'s account of the study notes that the commercials were divided into three groups based on the pre-test liking ratings ("well liked, disliked, indifferently received") and this classification was used in assigning treatments to subject groups. This would seem to imply that the much discussed smooth J-shaped curve was interpolated from data on only three levels of liking ratings.[2] Unfortunately, the document describing Schwerin's subsequent research which presumably demonstrated that the _same_ curvilinear relationship also

held for the liking and <u>remembering</u> of regular radio commercials is no longer available.[3]

The idea that attention value and remembering may increase with disliking has considerable common sense appeal. Drawing audience attention to advertising is not easily accomplished. The problem is especially difficult for broadcast media where large portions of the audience engage in other activities while viewing and/or listening. Steiner's (1966) observational study of television viewing behavior showed that less than half the audience paid full attention to commercials. Recently, Bither (1972), Gardner (1970) and Venkatesan and Haaland (1968) have conducted studies where the audience's attention has been manipulated or distracted away from the advertising message. The results indicate that learning and recall are sensitive to distraction. The intrusiveness of advertising is one of the most common complaints registered about it. Bauer and Greyser (1968, p. 244) found that this factor was mentioned for 63 percent of all radio advertising judged annoying by consumers and for 46 percent of all television commercials so classified. One can imagine tabulations of reasons why audiences find advertising annoying or unpleasant serving as a basis for developing a checklist of attention-getting techniques.

The rationale for the law of extremes noted in the above discussion emphasizes attention and remembering as response criteria. Subsequent stages in the response process also had to be taken into account. The critical assumption made in this regard was that any negative feelings aroused by irritating advertising will be either only momentary or at worst, directed toward the advertising but not associated with the advertised product, at least by the time of purchase (Wolfe, 1949, pp. 549-550, Devoe, 1956, p. 485). Evidence of a similar process has been found in

research on the over time pattern of effects of communications from sources of high and low credibility. Studies by Hovland and Weiss (1951) and Kelman and Hovland (1953) suggest that with the passage of time, the likelihood of spontaneously associating content of a communication with its source tends to decline. The operation of such a mechanism is crucial to the case made for a law of extremes because as one of its chief proponents pointed out, it serves "to explain how a 'disliked' commercial can avoid doing more harm than good" (Wolfe, 1949, p. 485). Thus it has been argued that irritating techniques facilitate attention and memory and the benefits of such learning will persist until the time of purchase because with the passage of time there is a tendency to disassociate the advertisement from the product advertised.

The proponents of the curvilinear hypothesis typically recognized that there were likely to be some sorts of limits on the types and range of dislike or unpleasantness over which commercially positive or desirable effects could be obtained. Wolfe (1949) cautioned against being "blatantly insulting" and stressed that irritating commercials had to be "skillfully planned." He was willing to concede that "while irritation advertising can sell goods, it cannot sell goodwill for the sponsor" (Wolfe, 1949, p. 487). Significantly, authors like Wolfe do not seem to have considered how repeated exposure to unpleasant advertisements might alter these relationships. This is somewhat surprising in light of the fact that repetition is an integral part of the irritation technique. As will be discussed in a later section, there are reasons for expecting that repetition reduces the likelihood of the advertised product being disassociated from its advertising.

The Superiority of the Pleasant Hypothesis

The merit of emphasizing "positive" as opposed to "negative" appeals, and thereby arousing pleasant rather unpleasant "feeling tone" was one of

the prime concerns of those who pioneered the field of advertising psychology. Most appear to have favored the former approach over the latter (Lucas and Benson, 1929). This point of view managed to persist despite much controversy. The arguments offered to support it have tended to shift over the years in response to the challenge posed by the law of extremes hypothesis.

A rationale frequently mentioned for the superiority of the pleasant thesis is the proposition that pleasant experiences are better remembered than unpleasant ones. To support this contention, advertising psychologists have sometimes appealed to the Freudian notion of repression (active forgetting of unpleasant experiences) or Thorndike's "law of effect" (connections between a stimulus and a response are strengthened or "stamped in" by satisfying experiences and weakened or "stamped out" by unpleasant or annoying ones) (Hattwick, 1950, p. 247; Poffenberger, 1932, p. 363). Other advocates of the superiority of the pleasant thesis appear to have viewed the relationship between affect and _remembering_ as U- or J-shaped rather than as a simple positive monotonic one. That is, in some of these discussions it was acknowledged that psychological research indicates that _memory_ is related to both intensity and direction of affect (Rapaport, 1961). However, this idea was typically discounted by stressing that although unpleasant ads are better than neutral ones, pleasant ads are best of all (Hattwick, 1950, p. 248; Britt, 1955, p. 32). Aside from the fact that experimental results do not justify any such simple generalization (Kanungo and Dutta, 1966), the hazards of making the leap from psychological theory to advertising practice were not explicitly considered.

Moving to the acceptance or attitude change level of response, we find another line of reasoning has been put forth to support the proposition

that pleasant advertising is more effective than the opposite variety. Here it is argued that the favorable or unfavorable affect consumers experience as a result of the advertising will be transferred or carried over to the product advertised (Strong, 1925, p. 276). If the consumer dislikes the advertising, so the argument runs, then he will tend to dislike the product advertised and may refuse to purchase it. Weschler, in taking a strong stand against the law of extremes, argued as follows

> Psychological testing, common sense, and logical thinking all convince us that there is no dis-association in the listeners' mind between their dislike of the commercial message itself and of the product advertised. On the contrary, it is accepted fact that emotions, pleasant or unpleasant, tend to become associated with the total situation in which they are experience and with all of the parts which make up that situation (Wechsler, 1945, pp. 36-37).

Here we see an explicit rejection of the advertising-product dissociation hypothesis espoused by proponents of the law of extremes.

Immediate Versus Delayed Effects

The major point on which the two theories are clearly contradictory involves the question of whether or not affective reactions aroused by an advertising treatment are transferred to the product featured in the advertisement. Drawing upon concepts from attitude change research which point to the importance of distinguishing between immediate and delayed effects of a communication, we can identify a possible basis for reconciling the seemingly conflicting views held on this matter. More specifically, we suggest that there are grounds for expecting the superiority of the pleasant hypothesis to hold for measures of attitude change taken immediately after exposure while the law of extremes hypothesis should apply to delayed measures of persuasive impact.

Research on source credibility and the sleeper effect (e.g., Hovland

and Weiss, 1951; Kelman and Hovland, 1953) suggests that the elapsed
time between exposure and measurement may be a critical factor for the
problem under consideration here. For the purposes at hand, the basic
ideas may be described as follows· as the interval from exposure to
measurement lengthens, the tendency for the communication source and
content <u>not</u> to be spontaneously associated increases, giving rise to
different patterns of attitude change over time for high and low credibility sources.

It would seem reasonable to predict that immediately after exposure,
the opportunity for feelings evoked by an advertisement to carry-over or
influence product attitudes is maximal. At that time, the persuasive
impact of an advertisement should be enhanced by its pleasantness or
likability but adversely affected by unpleasantness and dislike, an out-
come· that would conform with the superiority of the pleasant hypothesis.
In his review of attitude change research on liking and persuasion,
McGuire (1969, pp. 192-193) notes that most consistency theories would
predict a positive relationship between these two variables and he cites
some empirical support for such. However, if a dissociation process
similar to that posited for the sleeper effect begins to operate as
time since exposure increases, then spontaneous connections between
product and advertising become less likely and the initial advantage of'
pleasant advertising over unpleasant advertising should be reduced or
removed entirely--a result compatible with the law of extremes hypothesis.

The meaning and empirical status of the sleeper effect hypothesis
have recently been subjected to some critical re-analyses. Gillig and
Greenwald (1972) and Capon and Hulbert(1973) have pointed out that
various conceptions of what constitutes a sleeper effect have been employed in past studies of the phenomenon. The sleeper effect was originally

defined as a delayed _increase_ in the persuasive impact of a communica=
tion from a source _low_ in credibility. Such a result contrasted with
the _decrease_ over time generally observed for the effect of a message
from a source _high_ in credibility.. Combining these two patterns would
show that whereas the impact of the high credibility source was greater
than the low credibility source immediately after exposure, this difference
in effectiveness would decline or even disappear altogether with the
passage of time (Hovland and Weiss, 1952; Kelman and Hovland, 1953).
As research in this area progressed, the empirical criterion of the
sleeper effect shifted from the original notion of a _delayed increase_
in the persuasive impact of a _low_ credibility source to that of an
interaction effect between source credibility (high versus low) and time
of the post-exposure measure (immediate versus delayed) (e.g., Watts
and McGuire, 1964). Various over time patterns of effect of high and
low credibility sources could satisfy the latter criterion but would
be inconsistent with the former (Capon and Hulbert, 1973). In fact,
Greenwald and Gillig (1971, p. 7) contend that, "There is no published
report of a sleeper effect in which the increase in opinion from an immediate to a delayed posttest is statistically reliable."[4] They go on
to point out that evidence from previous studies as well as that
developed in a series of experiments they conducted indicates that,
"There is a significant interaction between source credibility and
time of opinion posttest, but this interaction is almost totally dependent on the loss of effect of the high-credible source, not an increase in effect of the low-credible source."

The explanation generally offered for the sleeper effect is that as
the time since exposure increases, the content of a communication is less

likely to be spontaneously associated with its source (Hovland, Janis, and Kelley, 1953, p. 255; McGuire, 1969, p. 259).[5] It is important to recognize that this dissociation hypothesis does not imply that the persuasive impact of a low credibility source will necessarily increase over time (Gillig and Greenwald, 1972). The type of interaction noted above, which Greenwald and Gillig (1971) suggest is reliable, can also be accounted for by the dissociation hypothesis. If processes like this "revised" sleeper effect and dissociation phenomena operate in the case of consumer response to pleasant and unpleasant advertising, then we would expect to find that the nature of the liking-effectiveness relationship would be different for immediate and delayed measures of effect. (Delayed measures are of greater significance to advertisers than immediate post-exposure ones inasmuch as some period of time ordinarily lapses between exposure to advertising and the occasion of purchase when product perceptions and attitudes become activated.

The Effects of Repetition

It would appear that making the distinction between immediate and delayed response allows us to argue that the law of extremes and the superiority of the pleasant hypotheses are not necessarily incompatible only with reference to effects predicted after a single exposure. Repeated exposure to the same message makes the picture more complicated.

Some have suggested or implied that repeated exposure to irritating advertising will increase the likelihood of adverse reactions to the advertising being transferred to the advertised product (Hepner, 1964, pp. 430-431; Seehafer and Laemmar, 1959, p. 236). Weinberger (1961) has expressed the view that the sleeper effect is not likely to occur in advertising situations because repeated exposure to the same advertisement will diminish the tendency for a product to be disassociated from its

advertising. Subsequent exposures should serve to reinforce the affective
reaction elicited by the initial exposure and thereby increase spontaneous
association of a product with its advertising. Such an occurence would
be consistent with the results from Kelman and Hovland's (1953) study of
source effects which demonstrated that a "reinstatement" of the source
at the time of a delayed measurement of opinion change counteracted the
sleeper effect. That is, when subjects were reminded of the communication
source (but not re-exposed to its content) some time after the first
exposure, there was a persistence of a significant source effect similar
to that observed immediately after the original exposure.

Repetition may involve still other processes about which there is
some disagreement. Weiss (1966) cites evidence from psychological
research to support his suggestion that under conditions of "low motiva-
tion to buy or learn" (which would be expected for broadcast advertising
of package goods - Krugman, 1967), attention diminishes with repetition
He also suggests that "repeated presentation of an emotionally provocative
stimulus leads to a kind of affective adaptation and reduction of arousal"
and notes that "this kind of neutralizing of affective properties occurs
whether the affect initially aroused is positive or negative" (Weiss, 1966,
p. 421). Hence, such affective adaptation might operate to reduce the
magnitude of the "source reinstatement" effect brought about by repetition

Others have expressed a somewhat different view from that put forth
by Weiss. Krugman (1961) conjectured that "soft sell" television commercials benefit more from repetition than the "hard sell" variety.
Weilbacher (1970) argues that repetition produces different "life cycles"
for advertisements, depending upon the nature of their affective quality.
Specifically, he (p. 221) hypothesizes that whereas "the informativeness

and entertainment of a particular advertising communication may be,
at best, transitory and short lived" but "annoyance and offense in
advertising is inherently cumulative." The fact that repetition is
typically near the top of the list of reasons consumers most frequently
mention for finding broadcast advertising annoying (e.g., Bauer and
Greyser, 1968) would seem to be consistent with the latter hypothesis.
Controlled studies of the influence of repetition on the affectivity of
advertising stimuli are conspicuously absent in the available literature.
Grass and Wallace (1969) have reported data from a field study which
indicated that the favorability of attitudes toward a set of television
commercials that were initially well-liked declined somewhat over the
course of a year-long campaign in which the commercials were repeated.

Sawyer's review of the psychological research on repetition that
appears elsehwere in this volume identifies some additional areas of
complexity. Grounds for resolving the issues noted here would seem to
be presently lacking.

In summary then, we find in the advertising literature two competing theories about the relationship between advertising affect and
its persuasive impact. The question of whether the relationship is
curvilinear or a monotonic increasing one has been the subject of
considerable previous debate. These two points of view have never been
precisely formulated, and several key matters are left ambiguous. The
concept of affect has not been clearly defined in either theoretical
or operational terms. There has been no explicit recognition of media
differences. One might be tempted to suggest the superiority of the
pleasant school of thought has merely focused its attention on a limited
range of the more general curvilinear or J-shaped relationship advocated
by the proponents of the law of extremes. However, such a simplistic
attempt at integration would overlook the fact that the two theories

postulate quite different intervening processes at both the message attention/remembering and product attitude change or acceptance stages of communications response. Analysis of the problem from the point of view of attitude change research suggests that delayed reaction and repetition effects are likely to be critical factors affecting the advertising liking-persuasion relationship.

Thus far, the discussion has focused on theoretical perspectives and issues. We now consider what light the available empirical evidence can cast on the questions raised by the foregoing analysis. As will be evident from the review presented in the next section, the number of pertinent studies found in publicly available sources is limited. One suspects that much relevant data has been gathered in proprietary pre-testing studies but remains unanalyzed and outside the public domain.

EMPIRICAL STUDIES OF RESPONSE

Various pieces of evidence bearing on the relationship between the affective quality of advertisements and their persuasive impact are to be found in the published advertising research literature. In the foregoing discussion we saw that different views have been expressed about the nature of the intervening process that operates to link advertisement affect to effectiveness. Consequently, in examining empirical results we are especially interested in distinguishing among measures that relate to different stages or levels in the advertising response process. The "attention-comprehension-acceptance" framework of attitude change research provides a useful basis for organizing our review of the available research. Unfortunately, none of the studies uncovered measured more than one level of response. Given the nature of the material available, it will be convenient to consider first findings that relate to the attention-

comprehension phases (advertisement recognition and recall measures) which
are grouped together under the heading of "reception." Regarding the
acceptance stage, we discuss results based on attitudinal and behavioral measures of
measures of response separately.

<u>Advertisement Reception</u>

As noted previously, a number of advertising texts (Hepner, 1964, p 431,
Lucas and Britt, 1950, p. 381; Wolfe, 1949, p. 484) state that the Schwerin
Corporation found in its studies of <u>radio commercials</u> that liking and
<u>remembering</u> were related in a manner <u>similar</u> to that represented by the
J-shaped curve which Horace Schwerin employed to describe the relationship
between soldiers' liking of messages broadcast in mess halls and their
persuasion impact measured in terms of the extent to which the soldiers
actually engaged in the recommended <u>behavior</u>. Inasmuch as none of the
details of this work appear to have been preserved, we must look to other
sources for detailed evidence regarding the relationship between advertisement affect and attention or learning.

A subject which received a great deal of attention from the early
advertising psychologists was the question of the relative value of
"positive" and "negative" advertising appeals. The former type of stimuli
was seen as creating a pleasant and the latter an unpleasant "feeling tone"
among the audience. In 1929-30, Lucas and Benson (1929, 1930a, 1930b)
published a series of studies on this topic. They defined a positive
advertising appeal as one "directed toward the attainment of something
which is desirable" while a negative appeal "aims toward the avoidance
of an annoying or repulsive situation (Lucas and Benson, 1930c, p. 112).
To illustrate the difference between the two approaches, they reproduced
a pair of print ads for Pebeco tooth paste (Lucas and Benson, 1930c, pp. 113-114).
One carried the headline "Admired everywhere--the radiant smile that shows

the Mouth of Youth" and featured an intimate scene between an attractive
young couple. The other ad began with "I had six teeth pulled this
morning" and showed a man holding his jaw in obvious discomfort.

One of the studies conducted by Lucas and Benson (1930a) consisted
of a laboratory experiment. A group of 108 adult subjects were exposed
for 45 seconds to each of 15 positive and 15 negative magazine ads
matched with respect to size and the use of color but featuring 30
different products. Details were not reported concerning how the
positive versus negative appeal distinctions were made. Unaided and
then aided recall measures were obtained immediately after exposure to
the entire set of ads.

Total recall scores were calculated for the two groups of ads by
aggregating correct responses over ads and subjects. Differences were
small and inconsistent across the two measures. The unaided recall
measure for the negative appeal ads was six percent higher than that
for the positive appeal ads, but the reverse was true for the aided
recall data. Men and women appeared to react similarly. Lucas and
Benson repeated the study with a hundred junior and senior high school
students. Overall, the positive appeal ads were better recalled (on
both the unaided and aided measures) than the negative appeal ads, but
important sex and age interactions were evident. The recall differential
appeared greater for junior as compared to senior high school students,
and boys were more affected than girls.

A second study of interest here is that reported by Rudolph (1947).
"Feeling tone" was one of several variables he examined in his analysis
of factors affecting Starch recognition scores for some 2500 ads (one
half page or larger) that had appeared in the Saturday Evening Post in
the five year period between 1935 and 1939. Five judges rated the

feeling tone of the illustration contained in each ad by categorizing
it as "pleasant", "neutral", or "unpleasant " Sets of three ads
matched with respect to brand advertised and mechanical variables were
then identified with each set containing one ad that fell into each of
these three feeling tone categories. Recognition scores reflecting the
percentage of issue readers claiming to have seen the illustration
were then compared for ads possessing the conventional picture-caption-
copy format. In each triplet, the recognition score for the neutral ads
was taken as a reference value (100) and the scores for the pleasant
and unpleasant ads were expressed as ratios to that base. Unfortunately,
the only information presented was an "index of attention" obtained by
averaging these ratios across all triplets studies. The exact number
was not reported. The average attention index figures found for the
pleasant, neutral, and unpleasant ads were 106.7, 100, and 114.4, respectively. Interestingly, the pattern of these results is the reverse of
the J-shaped relationship suggested by Schwerin's law-of-extremes/curve-
of-remembrance discussed earlier. A separate analysis was done for
ads with a "comic strip" format. By their nature, none were "unpleasant"
and hence the only comparison possible was between the pleasant and neutral
categories. Pleasant ads scored higher than neutral ones with respect to
both attention value (of illustrations) and copy readership.

A third study deserving mention in this section is that due to Wells
(1964b). In the course of developing his "Emotional Quotient" (EQ) and
"Reaction Profile" (RP) scales for pretesting print advertisements, Wells
had respondents rate various ads using these instruments. For several
different sets of advertisements, he has reported correlations between the
average scores ads received on these scales and recall measures obtained
from different samples at the time the ads were actually run. For

example, the correlation between EQ and Gallup and Robinson Proved Name
Registration scores was found to be 59 (p < .05, one tail test) for eleven
black and white ads for the same product (Wells, 1964b, p. 47) For twenty
of the ads studied in the Advertising Research Foundation's Study of Print
Advertising Rating Methods (PARM), the "attractiveness" items of the RP
scale correlated .55 with recognition scores (p < .01, one tail test) and
.31 (p > 05, one tail test) with recall scores (Wells, 1964a, p 6).

Other analysis by Wells also indicated that recall can be affected by
attractiveness-meaningfulness interactions. Eleven pairs of ads from
the PARM study were examined, each pair matched according to their mean-
ingfullness ratings. He notes that "In nine of these cases, the _less_
attractive ad received the higher recall score in the PARM Study" and
he adds that "This was true in spite of the fact that high attractiveness
ratings generally went with high recall (Wells, 1964a, p. 8). The explanation suggested by Wells was that meaningfulness ratings are "contaminated"
by an ad's attractiveness; respondents overestimate the meaningful
of attractive ads and underestimate it for unattractive ads.

Clearly, no simple relationship between affect and attention or
learning emerges consistently from these studies. If one is willing to
infer a smooth curve from three data points, then Rudolph's findings
for magazine advertisements which were derived from the largest of the
three data bases can be viewed as a curvilinear relation and therefore
partly in accord with the J-shaped liking-remembering curve which Schwerin
reportedly found for radio commercials.

It might be argued that affect is likely to have a greater impact on
memory for broadcast commercials than for print advertisements because
broadcast media are more intrusive than print. As well, there is the

possibility that in a small sample of ads such as those studied by Lucas
and Benson and Wells, the variance among ads with respect to affect is
too limited to tap enough of both extremes of the positive-negative affect
continuum where, according to Schwerin, the effects become pronounced   On
the other hand, Wells' data indicate that liking-recall relations can be
affected by other cognitive reactions as well. Given this possibility,
correlational findings based on data aggregated over many ads tend to
be highly ambiguous at best.

Attitudinal Effects

        As part of their television commercial testing procedure, the
Schwerin Corporation routinely collected data pertaining to both the
audience's "liking" of commercials and their impact--the latter being
measured by the pre-post shift in preferences for the advertised products.[6] From time to time references to the relationship between these
two measures were mentioned in the Bulletin published monthly for several
years by the company. The November, 1962 issue summarized their findings
as follows:

> Research on more than 20,000 commercials indicates
> no observable relationship between liking and moti-
> vating effectiveness except at the extremes (Schwerin
> Research Corporation, 1962, p 2).

This statement was accompanied by a bar chart which showed mean effectiveness
index values of 133 for the "50 best liked" commercials, 100 for the "average"
commercial, and 77 for the "50 least liked" commercials. While no details
are given as to how the calculations were made, the above numbers, taken
literally, shows that effectiveness increased monotonically with liking.
As such, these data obviously contradict the notion of a "law of extremes"
and a J-shaped liking-effectiveness relationship. It is interesting
to note that certain other more disaggregated data reported by the Schwerin
organization also indicated a monotonic rather than a curvilinear relation-

ship. For example, liking and effectiveness scores for eleven British
catfood commercials were found to correlate .94 and non-linearities were
not suggested by an accompanying scatter diagram (Schwerin Research Corporation, 1963, p. 2).

This is one of those rare instances in advertising research where
something quite close to an independent replication study is available.
As part of a larger investigation of attitudes toward advertising (commissioned
by the Institute of Practitioners in Advertising), the British Market
Research Bureau (1967) tested a sample of one hundred television commercials
using essentially the same procedures as those employed by Schwerin (Treasure
and Joyce, 1967, p. 21). The commercials were produced by ten different
agencies and had previously been aired on television. Five commercials
were shown to different audiences at twenty theatre sessions   A total
of 779 subjects participated in the study. The relationship between
liking and effectiveness was examined at two levels. The first analysis
took individual differences in liking into account. Respondents were
grouped according to how much they liked the commercials and for each
group an overall effectiveness score (total preference shifts for all
commercials) was determined. The results indicated a fairly smooth
positive relationship between liking and effectiveness. The second
analysis was performed using mean liking and effectiveness scores for
each commercial computed by averaging individual responses. The commercials were divided into quartiles based on their average liking scores and
the mean value of the effectiveness measure was determined for each quartile.
No clear relationship between liking and effectiveness was discernible.[7]
While differences in the effectiveness measures among the liking quartiles
were slight, the effectiveness measures tended to be lower for the best
liked, and most disliked commercials suggesting an _inverted_ U-shaped

liking-effectiveness relationship.

The fact that liking and effectiveness were positively correlated across individuals but no such relationship was found across commercials when the data were averaged over respondents draws attention to the hetereogenity of consumers' reactions to the same advertising material. Bauer and Greyser (1968, p. 12) observed the same phenomenon in their study of reactions to specific advertisements and emphasized that "One person's annoyance may be another's enjoyment." Inasmuch as both liking and effectiveness were measured via questionnaires administered on one occasion, the observed association between the two variables at the individual level may be largely the result of selective perception tendencies and common method variance. Correlations of this kind found in other studies are subject to a similar interpretation. Steadman (1969) found the favorability of respondents' attitudes toward the use of sexual illustrations in advertising to be strongly associated with their ability to recall correctly brand names of advertisements featuring such materials to which they had been exposed. Bauer and Greyser's data (1968, pp. 285-291) indicated that individuals who used a product and those who preferred a brand tended to be less likely to regard its ads as annoying or offensive and were more likely to regard them as informative and enjoyable.

The final study relevant here is one conducted by Daniel Yankelovich, Inc. (no date) for the ABC Radio Network. Seventy-five radio commercials representing a variety of presentation styles and product classes were presented in sets of eight to groups consisting of approximately fifty respondents. A total of 550 women and men participated. The commercials were aired without program context. Each commercial was rated on forty-six descriptive scales which a factor analysis revealed tapped eight dimensions

of consumers' perceptions. Respondents also indicated on a three point
scale how much the commercials stimulated their interest in buying the
advertised brands. Mean scores were calculated for each commercial on
the "stimulation of buying interest" scale and the eight commercial perception variables, one of which was labelled, "offense and alienation of
the listener." Cross tabulations were reported between the dichotomized
buying interest measure (above or below average) and a threefold cate-
gorization of each of the eight factor scores (above average, average,
and below average). All eight dimensions used to characterize the
commercials were markedly associated with stimulation of buying interest.
Commercials judged highest on "offense and alienation" tended to be
below average in stimulating buying interest.

Compared to the findings for attention and memory measures, these
results for commercial liking and product predispositions appear much
more consistent. Except for the aggregate analysis from the British
television study, all three bodies of data revealed positive affect-effectiveness relationships and hence do not support the notion of a law of extremes.
It should be noted however, that on all of these studies, the post
attitude measure was taken immediately after exposure. Hence, they
would not reflect the sleeper effect phenomenon. Any confidence inspired
by the apparent consistency of findings here must be tempered by the
realization that all the evidence reviewed is basically correlational
and therefore subject to the usual ambiguities concerning causal priorities.
The latter caution would seem particularly germaine in the present
situation since, as noted previously, selective perception and common
methods variance are plausible explanations for the commercial attitude-
product attitude correlations observed in the studies reviewed. Given
the nature of the design and modes of analysis employed in the Schwerin

and British studies, there is the possiblity that the results reflect regression artifacts (Campbell and Clayton, 1961).

The studies considered thus far have been largely cross-sectional ones, where the relationship between advertisement affect and some criterion of effectiveness was examined within a sample of ads using measures averaged over many respondents. Such designs clearly limit one's ability to control or detect important interactions. For instance, there are indications that program environment-commercial affect interactions influence response to television commercials (Axelrod, 1963; Crane, 1964; Kennedy, 1971). An example of the kind of confounding of effects that can occur in aggregate data is provided by Wheatley and Oshikawa's (1970) recent experimental study of the effectiveness of positive and negative advertising appeals in changing attitudes toward life insurance. Subjects (college students) were exposed to written copy which emphasized either the favorable consequences of owning life insurance (positive appeal) or the undesirable results of not being insured (negative appeal). The messages were essentially similar in all other respects. Pre-testing indicated that students did perceive the stimuli as the experimenters intended. Attitudes toward life insurance were measured before and after exposure to the advertising material by six items loading heavily on the evaluative factor of the semantic differential. The overall results showed that the group receiving the negative appeal shifted their attitudes slightly more than those exposed to the positive appeal. Wheatley and Oshikawa's main interest was in testing two hypotheses about interactions between appeals and individual differences with respect to pre-exposure anxiety levels. The latter was measured by a psychological instrument administered at the end of the experiment. However, Wheatley and Oshikawa claim that the scale used taps an enduring anxiety trait

and its measurement was not affected by exposure to the experimental
stimuli. They predicted that among low anxiety subjects, the negative
appeal would produce more attitude change than the positive appeal,
while the reverse would hold for high anxiety subjects.

The results were in the direction predicted, but not uniformly
significant. Stimulated by a suggestion made by Ray and Wilkie (1970),
Wheatley (1971) undertook a reanalysis of the data for the negative
appeal condition. In the course of examining the implications of social
psychological research on fear appeals (Leventhal, 1970) for marketing
communications, Ray and Wilkie noted there was reason to believe that
product users would respond differently than non-users to anxiety-
arousing messages. To test for this possibility, Wheatley re-ran his
analysis of the negative appeal results so as to estimate the separate
effects of both prior ownership and anxiety level on attitude change.
When he did this, he found that anxiety level made virtually no difference
but an ownership effect was discernible, being significant at the .10
level. It appeared that the attitude change induced by the negative
appeal occured primarily among non-owners. Insurance owners' attitudes
were essentially unaltered by the negative appeal and anxiety level
did not appear to affect response directly at all. It would have been
interesting to see the results of a similar analysis of the positive
appeal condition. The existence of such complexities serves to under-
score the limitations of cross-sectional studies in this area.

Behavioral Measures

Our search of the literature turned up only two relevant studies
where behavioral measures of response were employed. Coupon returns were
used in one case and sales results in the other. The studies in question

were part of the series of investigations Lucas and Benson carried out many years ago concerning the relative effectiveness of positive and negative appeals.[8]

In one investigation (Lucas and Benson, 1929), coupon returns were compared for 117 pairs of print ads. Each pair contained one ad featuring a positive appeal, while the other utilized a negative appeal. The positive-negative appeals discriminations were checked for thirty of the ads by a panel of judges and practically no disagreements were uncovered. Each pair of positive and negative ads were for the same product and had appeared in the same magazine at about the same time of the year. The ad pairs were also matched with respect to such format variables as size, position, and the use of illustration, color, headlines, and text The number of coupons returned in response to the positive and negative ads were compared for each matched pair separately. The overall results indicated no tendency whatsoever for one type of appeal to be more effective than the other: fifty-seven comparisons favored the positive appeal and exactly the same number favored the negative appeals--the other three cases were tied. Further analyses wherein the data were disaggregated by product category and magazine revealed no discrepancies from the above pattern of results.

Lucas and Benson's other study (1930b) was based on data from three different situations where both positive and negative appeals had been used and related sales information was available that permitted comparisons to be drawn. The first involved a correspondence school selling educational courses. Advertisements generated inquiries which were followed up by personal letters that led to some purchases. Sales traceable to specific ads were compared for twenty-eight pairs of print advertisements

matched with respect to format variables. For sixteen of the twenty-eight comparisons, better sales results were achieved with a positive appeal than with a negative one.

A field experiment conducted by the manufacturer of a proprietary medicine was the source of materials for a second case study. Campaigns (apparently in newspapers) using different appeals were tested for four months in different cities. Sales during the test period were compared with sales during the same period of the previous year. Positive and negative appeals were the bases of two of the campaigns tested. Sales increased 171 percent where the negative appeal was used while the positive appeal was accompanied by a 10 percent <u>drop</u> in sales. Lucas and Benson note that prior to the test, a group of "advertising experts" had rated the positive appeal as being superior to the negative one.

The third case described the experience of a mail order agency in selling a particular book. Although few details were presented, Lucas and Benson (1930b) reported that negative appeals were found to be more effective than positive approaches.

The conclusions Lucas and Benson drew from their series of studies were that no inherent advantage could be claimed for either approach, and that product differences and variability in response within each type of appeal needed to be recognized. Their findings were of considerable importance at the time they were published, because of widespread controversy surrounding the subject.

Overall, we find that the available empirical evidence can contribute little to clarifying much less resolving the basic issues surrounding the law-of-extremes versus the superiority-of-the-pleasant controversy. The only relationship appearing with any consistency was the monotonic one between commercial liking and product attitude, and as noted, several ambiguities surround those results. None of the studies included measures

for more than one level in the response process. Practically all the data
discussed for attention and memory were for print ads, while the only
materials uncovered measuring response at the attitudinal level dealt
solely with broadcast commercials. The critical matters of delayed action
and repetition effects appear to have received no attention at all. In
the course of discussing this work brief mention was made in passing of
several methodological problems. Perhaps the most basic difficulty here
is the lack of precise definition and control of the independent variable
in these studies. The crude judgmental classification of ads into "positive"
versus "negative" or "pleasant" versus "unpleasant" groupings and the
simple, one item "liking" scales we see employed in most of the above
studies stand in sharp contrast with other evidence such as that obtained
in factor analytic studies which indicates that consumers' perceptions of
advertising stimuli is highly multidimensional (Leavitt, 1970; Daniel
Yankelovich, Inc., no date, Wells, 1964b). Given such complexity,
experimentation would seem to be called for. In the next section, a pre-
liminary effort in this direction is reviewed.

AN EXPERIMENTAL STUDY OF "SOFT SELL" AND
"HARD SELL" RADIO COMMERCIALS

<u>Hypotheses</u>

The present authors conducted an experiment aimed at investigating
some of the unresolved issues in this area (Silk and Vavra, forthcoming).
The effects of a pleasant, "soft sell" radio commercial were compared with
those of an irritating, "hard sell" commercial for the same brand. The
following predictions were made with reference to the effects of <u>one</u> exposure:

     1. Brand awareness and advertising recall should be
         greater for the hard sell commercial than the
         soft sell commercial.

29

2. Attitudes held toward the advertised brand should be the same for the hard and soft sell commercials when measured after a period of time has lapsed following exposure.

3. Brand preference for the advertised product should be greater for the hard sell commercial than for the soft sell commercial when measured after a period of time has lapsed following exposure.

The rationale for the first prediction was that the features of the hard sell commercial which made it irritating would result in greater attention and remembering than the subtle mood technique of the soft sell commercial. The second hypothesis was derived from the assumption that the dissociation process suggested by attitude change research on the sleeper effect would be operative here. The final prediction followed from the first two. Given that the hard sell commercial would attract more attention and produce more learning and remembering and at the same time not suffer any adverse effects through unfavorable reactions to the commercial being transferred to the product, then the hard sell commercial should produce more frequent selection of the advertised product as the preferred brand than the soft sell commercial. In addition to testing the above hypotheses regarding the effects of a single exposure, a two exposure condition was added to the design for both the hard and soft sell commercials. Given the unsettled questions noted earlier regarding the various possible ways that repetition might influence liking-effectiveness relationships, there was no basis for formulating any unequivocal hypotheses about the comparative effectiveness of two exposures to hard and soft sell advertising. The only predictions that could be entertained here were that for either type of commercial, awareness and remembering measures should be greater after two exposures as compared to one.

30

<u>Method</u>

Two radio commercials were specially prepared for use in the experiment. The objective was to create two commercials which would evoke quite opposite types of affective reaction but which otherwise would be as similar as possible. In an attempt to accomplish this, we deliberately incorporated into the commercials certain features which previous studies of attitudes toward radio commercials had indicated were among the most frequently mentioned sources of consumers' favorable and unfavorable reactions. The result was two presentations whose differences in style are best conveyed by the phrases, "hard sell" and "soft sell." The hard sell presentation featured an announcer with a harsh voice and an aggressive, feverish delivery and used some extraneous sound effects to dramatize the copy. In contrast, the soft sell commercial presented an announcer with a calm, soothing voice against a background of subdued music. The two commercials were identical in other essential respects such as copy theme, claims made, frequency of mention of brand name, length (one minute), and loudness. The final tapes were prepared by announcers, recording technicians, and producers with prior professional experience who, at the time, were associated with the Theatre Arts Department of the University of California, Los Angeles. The product featured in the commercials was an established (but not the leading) brand of shoe polish. The desiderata in choosing the advertised product were that it be salient to the consumption patterns of our subjects (male undergraduates) but not the object of deeply entrenched existing attitudes which would make it difficult for the commercial to achieve any detectable effect after only one or two exposures.

To establish that the commercials were, in fact, perceived to be different in a manner consistent with our expectations, they were exposed

to a sample of ninety male undergraduates drawn from the same general
population as the subjects employed in the subsequent experiment. The
order in which the commercials were presented to subjects was systematically
rotated to balance order effects. After hearing each commercial, subjects
rated it on Wells' (1964b) Emotional Quotient (EQ) and Reaction Profile
(RP) scales.[9] Marked differences were found between the two commercials on
both scales. The mean ratings for the pleasant, soft sell commercial were
more positive than those for the irritating, hard sell commercial on all
twelve EQ items and for ten of the twelve RP items--the two reversals were
for "new, different-common, ordinary" and "lively-lifeless" where the
differences were not significant.

In developing the RP scale with print ad ratings, Wells (1964b)
found the items formed three factors which he labelled "attractiveness,"
"meaningfulness," and "vitality."[10] These might be interpreted as roughly
corresponding to three variables discussed in attitude change research.
In his review of research on this topic, McGuire (1969a, pp. 184-185)
makes passing reference to the hard-soft sell notion in discussing different components of source and message variables. A possible way to
describe the difference between the hard and soft sell approaches would
be in terms of source "liking," "objectivity" (low suspicion of
perceived intent to persuade), and "dynamism" or "intensity of delivery"
which bear some resemblance to "attractiveness," "meaningfulness," and
"vitality," respectively.[11] The items from the RP scale on which the
two commercials did not differ significantly were both from the vitality
factor Based upon this post hoc interpretation then, one might conclude
that the soft sell commercial was perceived as more attractive or better
liked, and more meaningful or objective but equally vital or dynamic

compared to the hard sell message.

The experimental design employed was an "after-only with control." There were five groups involved in the experiment. One pair of groups heard either the hard sell or soft sell commercial <u>once</u>. A second pair were exposed to one or the other commercial <u>twice</u>. The fifth group served as a control and only completed the questionnaire. The sample size totalled across all five groups was 170.

In order to approximate natural radio listening conditions under which an audience member controls how closely he attends to commercials, we employed a masking technique which assured that a subject was exposed to the radio broadcast containing the commercial but did not force or direct his attention to it.[12] Two authentic radio newscasts were taped which also contained two genuine commercials. The experimental commercial was inserted into the tape so it appeared to be the lead-in commercial for the second newscast. On the day of the experiment, the classes were visited by the experimenter who informed subjects that he was embarking on a study of audience perception of political bias in radio newscasts and   needed their help in getting a "feel" for the subject. Subjects were told that a tape would be played containing some newscasts, and after hearing it, they would be asked to fill out a short questionnaire. No mention was ever made of the commercials contained in the tape which appeared to be a natural part of the broadcast segment recorded. When the tapes had been played and the questionnaire completed, the experimenter thanked the class and left. The playing of the tape required about twelve minutes and the entire procedure took approximately twenty to twenty-five minutes. In the two exposure condition, the same experimenter returned two days after the first presentation and repeated the entire

procedure. This was done under the guise of checking to see whether or not perceptions of political bias in newscasts were stable.

Two days after exposure (first or second) data relating to the hypotheses were obtained via questionnaires. Measures were obtained only once for the repetition (two exposure) condition. Steps were taken to maintain the disguise attached to the original circumstances of the exposure and thereby to preserve subjects' naivete as to the true purpose of the experiment as long as possible. This was done by having subjects respond to a questionnaire allegedly concerned with college students' buying habits which asked various questions about several different products including shoe polish. The order in which the questions were asked was as follows: unaided brand and advertising awareness, brand preference, aided commercial recall, brand attitudes, and commercial recognition. Brand preference was measured by giving subjects a shopping list containing the names of several product categories including shoe polish and asking subjects to indicate which brand they would purchase. Sixteen semantic differential-type items were used to measure brand attitudes.

<u>Results</u>

The main results may be summarized as follows. The first and third hypotheses above were strongly supported. Brand awareness, recall of the commercial, and brand preference were significantly greater for the hard sell commercial than for the soft sell approach. In regards to the second hypothesis, no differences were found between the control group and either of the two commercial treatment groups. Thus, it appeared that neither of the commercials had a measureable impact on subjects' attitudes toward the brand after a single exposure.

The effects of repetition changed the above picture considerably In the case of brand awareness and advertising recall, the second ex-

posure significantly raised these measures over the levels achieved after a single exposure. However, the absolute magnitude of increases resulting from the second exposure tended to be greater for the soft sell commercial than for the hard sell version. After a second exposure, the hard sell commercial's initial advantage with respect to attention and remembering was still evident but had been reduced.

While repetition was found to have no statistically significant effect on brand attitude for either commercial, the trend of the data suggested that the incremental effect of the second exposure was positive for the soft sell commercial but negative for the hard sell presentation. The identical pattern of effects was evident in the brand preference data. For the soft sell commercial, repetition resulted in a statistically significant gain in brand preference, while no significant change occurred from one to two exposures for the hard sell commercial. Whereas the first exposure of the hard sell was found to have a greater impact on brand preference than was realized for the soft sell commercial, the difference disappeared after one additional exposure.

The fact that the hard sell approach with its seemingly built-in advantage with respect to attention value and memorability outperformed (with respect to brand preference) the soft sell on the first exposure suggest that at least initially there was no marked tendency for any negative affect aroused by the commercial to be transferred to the product. However, it would appear that repetition altered the response process. Although we emphasize it was only a non-significant, directional result, it appeared that repetition of the soft sell had a positive effect on brand attitudes, while repetition of the hard sell tended to affect attitudes adversely. With higher levels of repeat exposure, a more clear cut result

might have been obtained. Overall, these findings appear consistent with
Krugman's (1961) hypothesis that soft sell copy holds up better with repetition than does the hard sell. Ray and Sawyer (1970, p. 27) also found
some indication of this with their "grabber" and "non-grabber" print ads.

Perhaps then, as the proponents of the superiority-of-the-pleasant
thesis have claimed, with repetition affective reactions toward advertising
do tend to become associated with the advertised product. All this is a
highly speculative interpretation of the results obtained here inasmuch as
for none of the treatments were we able to detect a significant difference
in brand attitudes between an exposed group and the control. Both commercials appeared capable of producing effects at the bottom (awareness and
remembering) and top (brand preference) of the response hierarchy, but
nothing in between at the attitudinal level. Ray and Sawyer (1970) found
much the same thing in their more extensive repetition experiments. If
repetition were operating here in a manner equivalent to the "reinstatement of the source" phenomenon found in attitude change research, then
we would expect to find some differences in brand attitudes between the
groups hearing the commercials and the control. Here, we observed only
a hint of such differences developing after the second exposure. Some
further insights into the underlying process might have been ascertained
had immediate post-exposure measures of effect been obtained in addition
to the delayed ones The general subject of "post communication time
trends in attitude change", to use McGuire's (1969, p. 252) terminology,
deserves attention in future work and is relevant to a number of other
problem areas in advertising, including copy testing, competitive effects,
and media scheduling.

Another interpretation of these results would be to suggest that
they merely constitute one further indication of the inadequacies of our

models and measures of hierarchical processes of response to advertising. Fishbein and Ajzen (1972, pp. 517-522) have recently criticized attitude change researchers for not paying careful enough attention to all stages in the attention-comprehension-acceptance process and suggested directions for improvement. Reformulated views of the processes mediating persuasion have been put forth by Greenwald (1968) and Leventhal (1970). In the advertising field, Bauer (1967), Krugman (1967) and Wright (1973) have all proposed alternative models of the response process which do not assume the simple type of instrumental learning underlying the traditional hierarchical model. Different conceptions and measures of the dependent variables merit consideration in carrying out additional work in this area.

CONCLUSION

This paper began by noting some questions that are frequently asked about what bearing the affective quality of advertising has on its effectiveness. Two seemingly different points of view regarding how liking and effectiveness are related were identified in the advertising literature. One position--the law of extremes hypothesis--holds that the relationship is curvilinear, while the other--the superiority-of-the-pleasant hypothesis--maintains it is a monotonic increasing one. The analysis presented here has attempted to pinpoint the critical points of conflict and also to suggest bases for reconciling differences. Thus we have argued that the answer to questions about the relationship between affect and effectiveness will differ according to how effectiveness is specified with respect to stage in the response hierarchy, frequency of exposure, and the time interval between exposure and measurement of effect.

37

Our review of the relatively small number of relevant empirical studies available revealed no pattern of consistent, unambiguous results. A failure to recognize explicitly the multidimensional nature of the independent variable (affect), the absence of measures of multiple response levels, and a general inattention to interactions tends to characterize most of the past work done in this area. Problems of internal validity also plague the typical design employed here which has been a correlational one, using measures aggregated over individuals for a cross-sectional sample of ads.

As has been proven to be the case in communications research generally, progress in this problem area is likely to be achieved by focusing less of effects per se and more on the conditions under which a particular kind of effect may occur. Given the nature of the problems and complexities discussed here, experimental studies are needed. Careful definition and manipulation of the independent variable in affect-effectiveness studies is problematic because of the difficulty of creating alternative messages that differ only in specified ways. Efforts should be made to build upon the work that has been done in defining the dimensions of consumers' perceptions of advertising stimuli and to attempt to relate such dimensions to relevant concepts and insights from the social psychological research on attitude change. Such connections can be highly useful in formulating hypotheses to be tested experimentally. Interactions involving delayed action and repetition effects deserve high priority.

The external validity of such experiments is likely to be limited. Hence, it would be highly desirable for such investigations to be done with the framework of Ray's (1969) concept of a "research system" in mind so as to lay a foundation for movement from highly controlled, laboratory conditions to more natural field settings. The work described in this paper represents an attempt to initiate work along these lines Hopefully, it will be carried forward in the future.

Figure 1

THE SCHWERIN LIKING-EFFECTIVENESS CURVE

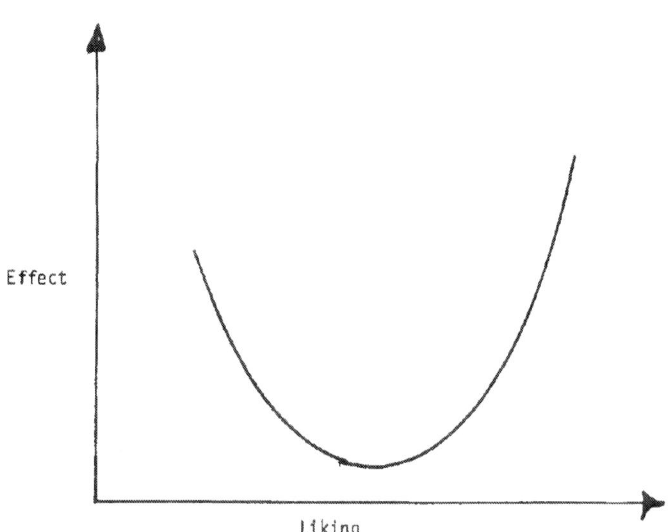

Source: Redrawn from (Schwerin Research Corporation, 1955, p. 3).

FOOTNOTES

[1]This figure has appeared in several advertising texts over the years.
For a recent example, see (Hepner, 1964, p. 431).

[2]According to information obtained by the authors from the Schwerin
Research Corporation, no detailed report of the study's methods and
results was ever published or otherwise made available generally.

[3]The source most often cited here is, How To Get More Out of Your Radio
Dollar, Schwerin Research Corporation, 1947. The authors have been
unable to locate a copy of this document.

[4]The appropriateness of the statistical methods employed in these
studies is suspect, especially the practice of relying on post
hoc rather than planned comparison tests. Capon and Hulbert (1973)
provide a detailed critique of the design of these investigations.

[5]Ray (1973, pp. 93-94) has advanced a learning theory explanation of
the sleeper effect. He argues that a communication's source will be
forgotten more rapidly than its content because the typical message is
more redundant with respect to content than source. However, Kelman and
Hovland's (1953) experiment (also see Watts and McGuire, 1964) indicated
that the critical requirement for the sleeper effect was not respondents'
ability to recall the source, but rather their spontaneous tendency to
associate source with content.

[6]See (Schwerin Research Corporation, 1959-60; or Buzzell and Kolin, 1964)
for a description of the procedures and materials used in the tests.

[7]No statistical test results were reported in (British Market Research
Bureau, 1967) or (Treasure and Joyce, 1967) for either of the analyses
summarized above.

[8]Lucas and Benson employed the same definitions of positive and negative
appeals here as those cited in the previous discussion of their work
concerned with recall measures.

[9]Wells originally developed these scales for use with print ads.
Some minor changes were made in the wording of the items to make them
suitable for eliciting ratings of radio commercials. At the time of the
study, these scales were the only established instruments available for
eliciting evaluations of advertising materials. More recently (Leavitt, 1970)
and (Wells, Leavitt, and McConville (1971) have reported development of
a reaction profile scale for television commercials. The factor
structure of television commercials ratings appears to be much more com-
plex than that for print ads.

40

[10]Wells (1964b) notes that these correspond to the evaluative, potency, activity dimensions of Osgood's semantic differential.

[11]The phrases "hard sell" and "soft sell" have been quite widely used both inside and outside advertising circles but never clearly defined. The only extended discussion of the two concepts known to the authors is that provided by Bursk (1947) in the context of personal selling.

[12]Belson (1953) utilized a similar procedure to study the effects on recall of changing the position of radio commercials. Politz (1961) has disguised the intent of his magazine advertising readership studies in essentially the same way.

REFERENCES

Abelson, Robert P., et al. (eds.) Theories of Cognitive Consistency.
Chicago: Rand McNally, 1968.

Axelrod, Joel. "Induced Moods and Attitudes Toward Products," Journal
of Advertising Research, 3 (June, 1963), 19-24.

Barban, Arnold M. "The Dilemma of 'Integrated' Advertising," Journal
of Business, 42 (October, 1969), 477-496.

Bauer, Raymond A. "Source Effect and Persuasibility: A New Look."
In Donald F. Cox (ed.) Risk Taking and Information Handling in Consumer
Behavior. Boston: Division of Research, Graduate School of Business
Administration, Harvard University, 1967, 559-578.

Bauer, Raymond A. and Greyser, Stephen A. Advertising in America: The
Consumer View. Boston: Division of Research, Graduate School of
Business Administration, Harvard University, 1968.

Belson, William A. "The Effect on Recall of Changing the Position of
a Radio Advertisement," Journal of Applied Psychology, 27 (May, 1953),
402-406.

Bither, Stewart W. "Effect of Distraction on the Persuasiveness of
Television Advertising," Journal of Marketing Research, 9 (February,
1972), 1-5.

British Market Research Bureau, Ltd. Attitudes to Television Advertising.
London: Institute of Practitioners in Advertising, June, 1967.

Britt, Steuart H. "How Advertising Can Use Psychology's Rules of Learning."
Printer's Ink, 252 (September,23, 1955), 74, 77, and 80.

Bursk, Edward C. "Low Pressure Selling," Harvard Business Review, 25
(Winter, 1947), 227-242.

Buzzell, Robert D. and Kolin, Marshall. Competitive Preference and Sales
Effectiveness. New York: Schwerin Research Corporation, October, 1964.

Campbell, Donald T. and Clayton, Keith N. "Avoiding Regression Effects
in Panel Studies of Communication Effect," Studies in Public Communication (Summer, 1961), 99-118.

Capon, Noel and Hulbert, James. "The Sleeper Effect: A Review and
Evaluation," Public Opinion Quarterly, 37 (Fall, 1973), in press.

Crane, Lauren E. "How Product, Appeal, and Program Affect Attitudes
Toward Commercials," Journal of Advertising Research, 4 (March, 1964), 15-18.

42

Devoe, Merrill. _Effective Advertising Copy._ New York: MacMillan, 1956.

Fishbein, Martin and Ajzeh, Icek. "Attitudes and Opinions." In Paul H.
Mussen and Mark R. Rosenzweig (eds.) _Annual Review of Psychology._
Palo Alto, California: Annual Reviews, Vol. 23, 1972, 487-544.

Gardner, David M. "The Distraction Hypothesis In Marketing." _Journal
of Advertising Research,_ 10 (December, 1970), 25-30.

Gillig, Paulette and Greenwald, Anthony G. "Is it Time to Lay the Sleeper
Effect to Rest?" Unpublished paper, no date.

Grass, Robert C. and Wallace, Wallace H. "Satiation Effects of TV
Commercials," _Journal of Advertising Research,_ 9 (September, 1969), 3-8.

Greenwald, Anthony G. "Cognitive Learning, Cognitive Response to
Persuasion, and Attitude Change." In Anthony G. Greenwald, Timothy C.
Brock, and Thomas M. Ostrom (eds.) _Psychological Foundations of
Attitudes._ New York: Academic Press, 1968, 147-170.

Greenwald, Anthony G. and Gillig, Paulette M. "A Cognitive Response
Analysis of the 'Sleeper Effect.'" Paper presented to the American
Psychological Association Division 8 Symposium on "Resistance to Per-
suasive Communication: Counterarguing Processes," Washington, D.C.,
September 4, 1971.

Greyser, Stephen A. "Irritation in Advertising," _Journal of Advertising
Research,_ 13 (February, 1973), 3-10.

Greyser, Stephen A. and Bauer, Raymond A. "Americans and Advertising:
Thirty Years of Public Opinion," _Public Opinion Quarterly,_ 30 (Spring,
1966), 69-78.

Greyser, Stephen A. and Reece, Bonnie B. "Businessmen Look Hard at
Advertising," _Harvard Business Review,_ 49 (May-June, 1971), 18-26
and 157-165.

Hattwick, Melvin S. _How to Use Psychology for Better Advertising._
New York: Prentice-Hall, 1950.

Hepner, Harry W. _Advertising._ 4th ed., rev. New York: McGraw-Hill, 1964.

Hovland, Carl I. and Weiss, Walter. "The Influence of Source Credibility
on Communication Effectiveness," _Public Opinion Quarterly,_ 15 (Winter,
1952), 635-650.

Hovland, Carl I., Janis, Irving L., and Kelley, Harold H. _Communication
and Persuasion._ New Haven, Conn.: Yale University Press, 1953.

Kanungo, Rabindra N. and Dutta, Satrajit. "Retention of Affective
Materials: Frame of Reference or Intensity?" _Journal of Personality and
Social Psychology,_ 4 (July, 1966), 27-35.

43

Kelman, Herbert C. and Hovland, Carl I. "'Reinstatement' of the Communicator in Delayed Measurement of Opinion Change," Journal of Abnormal and Social Psychology, 48 (July, 1953), 327-335.

Kennedy, John R. "How Program Environment Affects TV Commercials," Journal of Advertising Research, 11 (February, 1971), 33-38.

Krugman, Herbert E. "An Application of Learning Theory to TV Copy Testing," Public Opinion Quarterly, 26 (Winter, 1962), 626-634.

Krugman, Herbert E. "The Measurement of Advertising Involvement," Public Opinion Quarterly, 30 (Winter, 1967), 583-596.

Lazarsfeld, Paul F. and Field, Harry. The People Look at Radio. Chapel Hill, N.C.: University of North Carolina Press, 1946.

Lazarsfeld, Paul F. and Kendall, Patricia L. Radio Listening in America. New York: Prentice-Hall, 1948.

Leavitt, Clark. "A Multidimensional Set of Rating Scales for Television Commercials," Journal of Applied Psychology, 54 (May, 1970), 427-429.

Leventhal, Howard. "Findings and Theory in the Study of Fear Communications." In Leonard Berkowitz (ed.) Advances in Experimental Social Psychology. New York: Academic Press, Vol. 5, 1970, 119-186.

Lucas, D.B. and Benson, C.E. "The Relative Values of Positive and Negative Advertising Appeals as Measured by Coupons Returned," Journal of Applied Psychology, 13 (June, 1929), 274-300.

Lucas, D.B. and Benson, C.E. "The Recall Values of Positive and Negative Advertising Appeals," Journal of Applied Psychology, 14 (June, 1930), 218-238. (a).

Lucas, D.B. and Benson C.E. "Some Sales Results From Positive and Negative Advertising Advertisements," Journal of Applied Psychology, 14 (August, 1930), 363-370. (b)

Lucas, D.B. and Benson, C.E. Psychology for Advertisers. New York: Harper, 1930. (c).

Lucas, Darrell B. and Britt, Steuart H. Advertising Psychology and Research. New York: McGraw-Hill, 1950.

McGuire, William J. "The Nature of Attitudes and Attitude Change." In Gardner Lindzey and Elliot Aronson (eds.) Handbook of Social Psychology. 2nd ed. Reading, Mass: Addison-Wesley, Vol. 3, 1969, 136-314.

Poffenberger, Albert T. Psychology in Advertising. 2nd ed., rev. New York: McGraw-Hill, 1932

Politz Media Studies. The Rochester Study. New York: Saturday Evening Post, August, 1960.

Rapaport, David. _Emotions and Memory_. New York: Science Editions, 1961.

Ray, Michael L. "The Present and Potential Linkages Between the Microtheoretical Notions of Behavioral Science and the Problems of Advertising." Paper presented at the TIMS/University of Chicago Symposium on Behavioral and Management Science in Marketing, 1969.

Ray, Michael, L. "Psychological Theories and Interpretations of Learning," In Scott Ward and Thomas S. Robertson (ed.) _Consumer Behavior: Theoretical Sources_. Englewood Cliffs, N.J.: Prentice-Hall, 1973, 45-117.

Ray, Michael L. and Wilkie, William L. "Fear: The Potential of an Appeal Neglected by Marketing," _Journal of Marketing_, 34 (January, 1970), 54-62.

Ray, Michael L. and Sawyer, Alan G. "Repetition in Media Models: A Laboratory Technique," _Journal of Marketing Research_, 8 (February, 1971), 20-29.

Rosnow, Ralph L. "A 'Spread of Effect' in Attitude Formation." In Anthony G. Greenwold, Timothy C. Brock, and Thomas M. Ostrom (eds.) _Psychological Foundations of Attitudes._ New York: Academic Press, 1969, 89-108.

Rudolph, Harold J. _Attention and Interest Factors in Advertising._ New York: Funk & Wagnalls, 1947.

Schwerin Research Corporation. "Classic Study," _Schwerin Research Corporation Bulletin_, 3 (December, 1955), 2-4.

Schwerin Research Corporation. "The Effect of Variations in Test Conditions on the Reliability of the Competitive Preference Technique," _Technical and Analytical Review_, No. 3 (Winter, 1959-60), 1-25.

Schwerin Research Corporation. "SRC and the Sycophant Poets," _Schwerin Research Corporation Bulletin_, 10 (November, 1962), 1-3.

Schwerin Research Corporation. "Animal Ad Versions," _Schwerin Research Corporation Bulletin_, 11 (January, 1963), 1-3.

Seehafer, Gene F. and Laemmar, Jack W. _Successful Television and Radio Advertising._ New York: McGraw-Hill, 1959.

Silk, Alvin J. and Vavra, Terry. "An Experimental Study of Response to 'Hard' and 'Soft Sell' Radio Commercials." Working paper, Sloan School of Management, Massachusetts Institute of Technology, forthcoming.

Steadman, Major "How Sex Illustrations Affect Brand Recall," _Journal of Advertising Research_, 9 (March, 1969), 15-20.

Steiner, Gary A. _The People Look at Television._ New York: Knopf, 1963.

Steiner, Gary A. "The People Look at Commercials: A Study of Audience Behavior," _Journal of Business_, 39 (April, 1966), 272-304.

Strong, Edward K., Jr. *The Psychology of Selling and Advertising.* New York: McGraw-Hill, 1925.

Treasure, John and Joyce, Timothy. *As Others See Us.* London: Institute of Practitioners in Advertising, Occasional Paper 17, June, 1967.

Venkatesan, M. and Haaland, Gordon A. "Divided Attention and Television Commercials: An Experimental Study," *Journal of Marketing Research,* 5 (May, 1968), 203-205.

Watts, William A. and McGuire, William J. "Persistance of Induced Opinion Change and Retention of the Inducing Message Content," *Journal of Abnormal and Social Psychology,* 68 (February, 1964), 233-241.

Wechsler, Lewis S. "To Use or Not to Use the Irritaiion Technique in Radio Advertising," *Printer's Ink,* 223 (May 14, 1945), 36-37.

Weilbacher, W.M. "What Happens to Advertisements When They Grow Up," *Public Opinion Quarterly,* 34 (Summer, 1970), 216-223.

Weinberger, Martin. "Does the 'Sleeper Effect' Apply to Advertising?" *Journal of Marketing,* 25 (October, 1961), 65-68.

Weiss, Walter. "Repetition in Advertising." In Leo Bogart (ed.) *Psychology in Media Strategy.* Chicago: American Marketing Association, 1966, 59-65.

Wells, William D. "Recognition, Recall, and Rating Scales," *Journal of Advertising Research,* 4 (September, 1964), 2-8. (a).

Wells, William D. "EQ, Son of EQ and the Reaction Profile," *Journal of Marketing,* 28 (October, 1964), 45-51. (b).

Wells, William D., Leavitt, Clark and McConville, Maureen. "A Reaction Profile for TV Commercials," *Journal of Advertising Research,* 11 (December, 1971),11-17.

Wheatley, John J. and Oskikawa, Sadaomi. "The Relationship Between Anxiety and Positive and Negative Advertising Appeals," *Journal of Marketing Research,* 7 (February, 1970), 85-89.

Wheatley, John J. "Marketing and the Use of Fear or Anxiety-Arousing Appeals," *Journal of Marketing,* 35 (April, 1971), 62-64.

Wolfe, Charles Hull. *Modern Radio Advertising.* New York: Funk & Wagnalls, 1949.

Wright, Peter L. "The Cognitive Processes Mediating Acceptance of Advertising," *Journal of Marketing Research,* 10 (February, 1973), 53-62.

Yankelovich, Daniel, Inc. *The Yankelovich Report: A Media Research Program.* New York: Radio Network, no date.

www.ingramcontent.com/pod-product-compliance
Lightning Source LLC
LaVergne TN
LVHW051129190726
843642LV00003B/682